Learn I

Practical guide

A. De Quattro

Practical guide

1.Introduction to Rust

Rust is a very versatile and powerful programming language, created by Mozilla Research with the goal of providing programmers with an effective tool to create reliable, efficient, and secure software.

But what makes Rust so special and different from other programming languages? To answer this question, we need to examine some of the key features of Rust.

One of Rust's distinctive features is its advanced and innovative type system. Rust's type system is based on the concepts of "ownership" and "borrowing", which allows the compiler to guarantee the absence of memory leaks and data races during compilation. This means that Rust helps you write more robust and secure code from the development phase, without sacrificing performance.

Furthermore, Rust is a strongly typed language, which means you need to declare the type of every variable before using it. This may seem restrictive at first, but it will help you avoid many common errors that can occur during program execution.

Another interesting feature of Rust is its memory management system. Unlike other programming languages, Rust does not use a garbage collector to manage memory, but relies on a reference counting and borrowing mechanism that allows you to manage memory more efficiently and safely. This means that not only will your code be more performant, but also less susceptible to errors due to memory management issues.

Additionally, Rust offers a very powerful and secure concurrency system based on channels and threads. This system allows you to create multithreaded applications easily and safely, without having to worry about typical issues such as data races and deadlocks.

Another interesting feature of Rust is its clear and expressive syntax. Rust's syntax is very similar to that of C and C++, so if you are familiar with these languages, you should have no trouble learning Rust. However, Rust also has many advanced features that make it a very powerful and flexible language.

Finally, Rust is an open-source language, which means you can contribute to its development and improvement. The Rust ecosystem is rapidly growing, with a wide range of libraries and frameworks available to help you develop your applications faster and more efficiently. Rust is an innovative and powerful programming language that helps you write safer, more reliable, and efficient code. With its advanced type system, secure memory management, and powerful concurrency features, Rust is the ideal choice for developing complex and critical applications. If you are interested in learning a new programming language that allows you to take your skills to the next level, Rust might be the right choice for you.

2. Installation and Configuration of Rust Development Environment

Introduction

In this chapter, we will guide you through the process of installing and configuring Rust on your development environment. By the end of this chapter, you will have a fully functional Rust environment ready for writing and running Rust programs.

Prerequisites

Before we begin the installation process, make sure you have the following prerequisites:

1. An internet connection to download the necessary files.

2. A compatible operating system (Rust supports Windows, macOS, and Linux).

3. Basic familiarity with the command line.

Installation on Windows

If you are using Windows, follow these steps to install Rust on your machine:

1. Visit the official Rust website at https://www.rust-lang.org/tools/install to download the installer for Windows.

2. Run the installer and follow the on-screen instructions. Make sure to check the box that says "Add to PATH" during the installation process. This will add Rust to your system's PATH variable, allowing you to run Rust commands from the command line.

3. Once the installation is complete, open a command prompt and type `rustc --version` to check if Rust has been installed successfully. You should see the version number of Rust displayed on the screen.

Installation on macOS

For macOS users, the installation process for Rust is slightly different:

1. Open a terminal window and run the following command to download the installer script:

```sh

curl --proto '=https' --tlsv1.2 -sSf https://sh.rustup.rs | sh

```

2. Follow the on-screen instructions to install Rust on your machine. Make sure to select the default options during the installation process.

3. After the installation is complete, run the command `rustc --version` in the terminal to verify that Rust has been installed successfully.

Installation on Linux

If you are using a Linux distribution, you can install Rust using the following steps:

1. Open a terminal window and run the following command to download the installer script:

```sh
curl --proto '=https' --tlsv1.2 -sSf https://sh.rustup.rs | sh
```

2. Follow the on-screen instructions to install Rust on your machine. Make sure to select the default options during the installation process.

3. Once the installation is complete, run the command `rustc --version` in the terminal to confirm that Rust has been installed successfully.

Configuring Rust

Now that Rust is installed on your machine, you need to configure it to set up the Rust toolchain and manage your Rust projects.

Rustup

Rustup is the official Rust toolchain installer that allows you to easily manage different Rust versions and update the Rust compiler and standard library. To install Rustup, run the following command in your terminal:

```sh
curl --proto '=https' --tlsv1.2 -sSfS https://sh.rustup.rs | sh
```

Once Rustup is installed, you can use it to manage your Rust installations and toolchains. Here are some useful commands to get started with Rustup:

- `rustup update`: Updates the Rust compiler and standard library to the latest versions.

- `rustup toolchain list`: Lists the installed toolchains on your machine.

- `rustup default <toolchain>`: Sets the default

toolchain for your projects.

- `rustup target add <target>`: Adds a new target for cross-compiling Rust programs.

Cargo

Cargo is Rust's package manager and build system that allows you to easily manage dependencies, build, test, and run Rust projects. To install Cargo, make sure you have Rustup installed and run the following command in your terminal:

```sh
rustup component add cargo
```

Once Cargo is installed, you can use it to create new Rust projects and manage dependencies. Here are some useful commands to get started with Cargo:

- `cargo new <project_name>`: Creates a new Rust project with the specified name.

- `cargo build`: Builds the project in the current directory.

- `cargo run`: Builds and runs the project.

- `cargo test`: Runs the project's tests.

- `cargo doc`: Generates documentation for the project.

Setting up an IDE

While you can write Rust code in any text editor, using an Integrated Development Environment (IDE) can greatly improve your productivity. Here are some popular IDEs that support Rust:

1. Visual Studio Code: A lightweight and customizable IDE with support for Rust through extensions like Rust Analyzer.

2. IntelliJ IDEA: A powerful IDE with Rust support through the Rust plugin.

3. Atom: A hackable text editor with support for Rust through packages like ide-rust.

Choose an IDE that fits your workflow and install the necessary extensions or plugins to start writing Rust code in a more efficient way.

In this chapter, we walked you through the process of installing and configuring Rust on your development environment. By following the steps outlined in this chapter, you should now have a fully functional Rust environment ready for writing, building, and running Rust programs. In the next chapter, we will dive deeper into the Rust programming language and explore its features and capabilities.

3.Basic Syntax of Rust

Rust is a modern systems programming language that aims to provide a safe, concurrent, and practical option for developers. In this chapter, we will explore the basic syntax of Rust, covering concepts such as variables, data types, functions, control flow, and more.

Variables and Mutability

In Rust, variables are declared using the `let` keyword, followed by the variable name and optional type annotation. Variables in Rust are immutable by default, meaning that once a value is assigned to a variable, it cannot be changed. To declare a mutable variable, you can use the `mut` keyword before the variable name.

```rust
```

```
// Immutable variable

let x = 5;


// Mutable variable

let mut y = 10;


y = 15; // Valid, y is mutable
```

Data Types

Rust provides a variety of primitive data types, including integers, floating-point numbers, booleans, characters, and slices. Here are some examples of basic data types in Rust:

```rust
let a: i32 = 5; // Signed 32-bit integer
```

```rust
let b: f64 = 3.14; // 64-bit floating-point number

let c: bool = true; // Boolean

let d: char = 'a'; // Character

let e: &[i32] = &[1, 2, 3]; // Slice of integers
```

Rust also supports compound data types, such as tuples, arrays, and structs. Tuples are fixed-size collections of values, while arrays are fixed-size collections of homogeneous elements. Structs, on the other hand, are custom data types that allow you to define named fields.

```rust
// Tuple

let tuple: (i32, f64, bool) = (5, 3.14, true);


// Array
```

```rust
let array: [i32; 3] = [1, 2, 3];


// Struct

struct Point {

    x: i32,

    y: i32,

}


let point = Point { x: 10, y: 20 };
```
```

Functions


Functions in Rust are defined using the `fn` keyword, followed by the function name, parameters, return type, and body. Rust uses a lightweight syntax for defining functions, making it easy to read and write concise code.
```

```rust
fn add(x: i32, y: i32) -> i32 {

    return x + y;

}


fn main() {

    let result = add(5, 10);

    println!("Result: {}", result);

}
```

Rust also supports closures, which are anonymous functions that can capture their environment. Closures are useful for defining short, inline functions that can be passed as arguments or returned from other functions.

```rust
let add_closure = |x: i32, y: i32| -> i32 { x +
```

```
    y };

    let result = add_closure(5, 10);

    println!("Result: {}", result);
```

Control Flow

Rust provides several control flow constructs, including `if` expressions, `match` expressions, loops, and more. The `if` expression in Rust is similar to other programming languages, but with some special features, such as pattern matching and multiple arms.

```rust
let x = 5;
```

```
if x < 10 {

    println!("x is less than 10");

} else if x == 10 {

    println!("x is equal to 10");

} else {

    println!("x is greater than 10");

}
```

The `match` expression in Rust is a powerful feature that allows you to compare a value against a series of patterns and execute the corresponding block of code. This is similar to a `switch` statement in other languages, but with added flexibility and safety.

```rust
let y = 5;
```

```
match y {

    1 => println!("One"),

    2 => println!("Two"),

    _ => println!("Other"),

}
```

Rust also supports loops, including `loop`, `while`, and `for` loops. The `loop` keyword creates an infinite loop, which can be exited using the `break` statement. The `while` loop executes a block of code as long as a condition is true, while the `for` loop iterates over a collection of elements.

```rust

let mut n = 0;


loop {
```

```rust
        println!("n: {}", n);
        n += 1;


        if n == 5 {
            break;
        }
    }


    let mut i = 0;
    while i < 5 {
        println!("i: {}", i);
        i += 1;
    }


    for j in 0..5 {
        println!("j: {}", j);
    }
```

```
```

Error Handling

In Rust, errors are handled using the `Result` type, which represents either a successful result or an error. The `Result` type has two variants, `Ok` and `Err`, which can be used to propagate errors and handle them gracefully.

```rust
fn divide(x: i32, y: i32) -> Result<i32, &'static str> {
    if y == 0 {
        return Err("Division by zero");
    }

    Ok(x / y)
}
```

```rust
match divide(10, 2) {

    Ok(result) => println!("Result: {}", result),

    Err(error) => println!("Error: {}", error),

}
```

Rust also provides the `panic` macro, which can be used to terminate the program with a custom error message. The `panic` macro is typically used for unrecoverable errors, such as out-of-bounds array access or failed assertions.

```rust
fn find_element(array: &[i32], target: i32) -> i32 {

    for &element in array.iter() {

        if element == target {
```

```
        return element;

    }

  }


    panic!("Element not found");

}
```

In this chapter, we have covered the basic syntax of Rust, including variables, data types, functions, control flow, and error handling. Rust's syntax is designed to be concise, expressive, and safe, making it a powerful language for systems programming.

In the next chapter, we will dive deeper into Rust's features, such as ownership, borrowing, lifetimes, and more. Stay tuned for more in-depth discussions on how to write efficient and safe code in Rust.

4.Rust Variables and Data Types

One of the key features of Rust is its strong type system, which helps prevent common bugs and vulnerabilities in software. In this chapter, we will explore the various variables and data types available in Rust.

Variables in Rust

In Rust, variables are declared using the let keyword, followed by the variable name and an optional type annotation. Variables in Rust are immutable by default, which means that once a value is assigned to a variable, it cannot be changed. To declare a mutable variable, you can use the let mut keyword.

Here is an example of declaring a variable in Rust:

```rust
// Immutable variable

let x = 5;


// Mutable variable

let mut y = 10;
```

Data Types in Rust

Rust has a rich set of built-in data types that are classified into two categories: scalar types and compound types.

Scalar Types

Scalar types represent a single value and include integers, floating-point numbers, booleans, and characters.

Integer Types

Integers in Rust can be signed or unsigned and can have different sizes. Here are some of the integer types available in Rust:

- i8: 8-bit signed integer

- i16: 16-bit signed integer

- i32: 32-bit signed integer

- i64: 64-bit signed integer

- u8: 8-bit unsigned integer

- u16: 16-bit unsigned integer

- u32: 32-bit unsigned integer

- u64: 64-bit unsigned integer

Floating-Point Types

Floating-point numbers in Rust come in two flavors: f32 and f64, representing 32-bit and 64-bit floating-point numbers, respectively.

Boolean Type

The boolean type in Rust is denoted by the bool keyword and can have two values: true or false.

Character Type

Characters in Rust are represented by the char type and are enclosed in single quotes. Rust uses Unicode for character encoding, allowing for support for a wide range of characters.

Compound Types

Compound types can group multiple values

into a single entity and include tuples, arrays, and slices.

Tuples

Tuples in Rust are fixed-size collections of elements of different data types. They are declared using parentheses and can have any number of elements.

Here is an example of a tuple in Rust:

```rust
let my_tuple = (1, true, 'a');
```

Arrays

Arrays in Rust are fixed-size collections of

elements of the same data type. They are declared using square brackets and can contain a specified number of elements.

Here is an example of an array in Rust:

```rust
let my_array = [1, 2, 3, 4, 5];
```

Slices

Slices in Rust are references to a contiguous sequence of elements within a collection. They are denoted by a range of indices and can be used to access subarrays or subparts of arrays.

Here is an example of a slice in Rust:

```rust
let my_slice = &my_array[1..4];
```

Type Inference

Rust features type inference, which allows the compiler to determine the type of a variable based on its usage. This helps reduce the need for explicit type annotations and makes the code more concise and readable.

Here is an example of type inference in Rust:

```rust
let x = 5; // Compiler infers x as an integer
let y = 3.14; // Compiler infers y as a floating-point number
```

```
```

Type Conversion

Rust provides the as keyword to perform type conversion between different data types. Type conversion can be explicit or implicit, depending on the context.

Here is an example of type conversion in Rust:

```rust
let x: i32 = 5;

let y: i64 = x as i64;


let a: f32 = 3.14;

let b: i32 = a as i32;
```

Rust's strong type system helps prevent bugs and vulnerabilities in software, making it a robust and reliable programming language. By understanding the different types of variables and data types in Rust, you can write safer and more efficient code.

5.The operators in Rust

Rust is a modern systems programming language that focuses on safety, performance, and concurrency. One of the key features of Rust is its memory safety guarantees, which are enforced by the compiler at compile time. This allows developers to write fast and efficient code without worrying about common programming errors such as null pointer dereferences, buffer overflows, or data races.

In Rust, operators are used to perform operations on values. There are several types of operators in Rust, including arithmetic operators, bitwise operators, comparison operators, and logical operators.

Arithmetic operators are used to perform basic arithmetic operations such as addition, subtraction, multiplication, and division. In Rust, the arithmetic operators are the same as in many other programming languages, including the plus sign (+) for addition, the minus sign (-) for subtraction, the asterisk (*) for multiplication, and the forward slash (/) for division.

Bitwise operators are used to perform bitwise operations on integer values. Some common bitwise operators in Rust include the bitwise AND operator (&), the bitwise OR operator (|), the bitwise XOR operator (^), and the bitwise NOT operator (~). These operators are useful for manipulating individual bits in an integer value.

Comparison operators are used to compare two values and determine their relationship. In Rust, comparison operators include the equal to operator (==), the not equal to operator (!=), the greater than operator (>), the less than operator (<), the greater than or equal to operator (>=), and the less than or equal to operator (<=).

Logical operators are used to combine multiple Boolean expressions and evaluate them as a single Boolean value. In Rust, logical operators include the logical AND operator (&&), the logical OR operator (||), and the logical NOT operator (!). These operators are useful for combining multiple conditions in conditional statements and loops.

In addition to these basic operators, Rust also provides several compound assignment operators that combine an arithmetic or bitwise operation with an assignment operation. For example, the compound assignment operator += is equivalent to x = x + y, where x and y are variables.

One of the key features of Rust is pattern matching, which allows developers to destructure complex data structures and extract values based on their patterns. This can be useful when working with enums, structs, tuples, and other data types in Rust.

For example, consider the following code snippet that defines an enum called Shape and uses pattern matching to print the type of each shape:

```rust
enum Shape {
    Circle,
    Square,
    Triangle,
}

fn print_shape(shape: Shape) {
    match shape {
        Shape::Circle => println!("This is a circle"),
```

```rust
        Shape::Square => println!("This is a
square"),

        Shape::Triangle => println!("This is a
triangle"),

    }
}


fn main() {
    let circle = Shape::Circle;

    let square = Shape::Square;

    let triangle = Shape::Triangle;


    print_shape(circle);

    print_shape(square);

    print_shape(triangle);
}
```

In this example, the enum Shape defines three different shapes: Circle, Square, and Triangle. The print_shape function uses pattern matching to determine the type of each shape and prints a corresponding message.

Rust also supports operator overloading, which allows developers to redefine the behavior of operators for custom data types. This can be useful when working with user-defined types that require custom arithmetic, bitwise, or comparison operations.

For example, consider the following code snippet that defines a custom Point struct and overloads the addition operator (+) for adding two Point objects together:

```rust
use std::ops::Add;
```

```rust
#[derive(Debug)]
struct Point {
    x: i32,
    y: i32,
}

impl Add for Point {
    type Output = Point;

    fn add(self, other: Point) -> Point {
        Point {
            x: self.x + other.x,
            y: self.y + other.y,
        }
    }
}
```

```
fn main() {

    let point1 = Point { x: 1, y: 2 };

    let point2 = Point { x: 3, y: 4 };


    let sum = point1 + point2;


    println!("{:?}", sum);

}
```
```

In this example, the Point struct defines a custom data type for representing 2D points with x and y coordinates. The Add trait is implemented for the Point struct, which allows the addition operator (+) to be used for adding two Point objects together.


Rust also provides a range of built-in functions and methods for working with collections, strings, and other common data
```

types. These functions and methods can be used in combination with operators to perform complex operations efficiently.

For example, consider the following code snippet that uses the map method to apply a transformation to each element of a vector and the filter method to remove elements that do not satisfy a predicate:

```rust
fn main() {
    let numbers = vec![1, 2, 3, 4, 5];

    let squares: Vec<i32> = numbers.iter().map(|&x| x * x).collect();
    let evens: Vec<i32> = numbers.iter().filter(|&x| x % 2 == 0).cloned().collect();

    println!("{:?}", squares);
```

```
    println!("{:?}", evens);

}

```

In this example, the numbers vector contains a list of integers. The map method is used to square each element of the vector, and the filter method is used to select only the even elements. The results are collected into separate vectors and printed to the console.

Overall, operators play a crucial role in Rust programming by allowing developers to perform a wide range of operations on values efficiently. By understanding how to use operators effectively, developers can write clean, concise, and performant code in Rust.

6. The mutability of variables, constants, and visibility in Rust

One of the distinctive features of Rust is its static type system, which enforces strict rules to ensure that code is free of errors and unexpected behaviors. In this context, the mutability of variables, definition of constants, and management of visibility play a fundamental role in determining the structure and behavior of a Rust program.

In Rust, the mutability of variables is tightly controlled by the compiler to ensure that changes occur in a safe and predictable manner. This means that every variable in Rust is by default immutable, unless explicitly declared as mutable using the `mut` keyword. For example, the following statement defines a variable `x` as immutable:

```
```

```
let x = 5;
```

Here, `x` cannot be changed after its initialization. If an attempt is made to overwrite the value of `x`, the compiler will report an error. To allow modification of `x`, the variable must be declared as mutable:

```
let mut x = 5;
x = 10;
```

This time, the compiler will not display any errors, as the variable has been declared as mutable. The usage of mutability requires careful attention from the programmer, as it can lead to unexpected behaviors and errors if not handled correctly. However, mutability is often essential to allow for the modification of variable states within a Rust program.

Constants in Rust are defined using the `const` keyword and are of similar importance to the mutability of variables. Constants are immutable values that are evaluated at compile time and cannot be changed during program execution. Constants are declared in the global scope and must always be initialized with a constant value known at compile time. For example:

```
const PI: f32 = 3.14159;
```

In this case, `PI` is an immutable constant with an approximate value of the mathematical constant π. Constants are useful for defining values that should never change and for ensuring code consistency and predictability. Since constants are evaluated at compile time, they are embedded directly into the executable code and can be used in contexts where mutability is not desired.

The visibility of variables, constants, and functions in Rust is controlled by the use of the `pub` and `priv` keywords. These keywords determine whether an entity can be accessed inside or outside of the module in which it is defined. In Rust, code is organized into modules that serve as logical isolation units within a program. Elements defined within a module are not visible externally unless marked as public using the `pub` keyword.

For example, the following declaration defines a function `add` with the default visibility as private:

```
fn add(a: i32, b: i32) -> i32 {
```

```
    a + b

}

```

In this case, `add` can only be invoked within the module in which it is defined. To make the `add` function public and therefore accessible outside of the module, the `pub` keyword can be used:

```

pub fn add(a: i32, b: i32) -> i32 {

    a + b

}

```

After the modification, the `add` function can be called from other modules within the Rust program. Managing visibility is crucial for organizing code in a modular way and compile time, they are embedded directly into the executable code and can be used in contexts where mutability is not desired.

The visibility of variables, constants, and functions in Rust is controlled by the use of the `pub` and `priv` keywords. These keywords determine whether an entity can be accessed inside or outside of the module in which it is defined. In Rust, code is organized into modules that serve as logical isolation units within a program. Elements defined within a module are not visible externally unless marked as public using the `pub` keyword.

For example, the following declaration defines a function `add` with the default visibility as private:

```
fn add(a: i32, b: i32) -> i32 {
```

```
    a + b

}
```

In this case, `add` can only be invoked within the module in which it is defined. To make the `add` function public and therefore accessible outside of the module, the `pub` keyword can be used:

```
pub fn add(a: i32, b: i32) -> i32 {

    a + b

}
```

After the modification, the `add` function can be called from other modules within the Rust program. Managing visibility is crucial for organizing code in a modular way and ensuring a healthy separation of responsibilities within a project.

The mutability of variables, definition of constants, and management of visibility are crucial aspects of programming in Rust. Mutability ensures the correctness and predictability of changes to variable states, while constants allow for the definition of immutable values at compile time. Visibility controls access to entities within and outside of modules, contributing to better organization and structuring of code. Understanding and correctly utilizing these concepts is essential for writing efficient and reliable code in Rust.

Variables in Rust can be divided into two main categories: immutable variables and mutable variables. Immutable variables are those whose assignment cannot be changed once they have been defined, while mutable variables can be modified after their initial assignment.

To declare a variable in Rust, you need to use the keyword "let" followed by the name of the variable and the data type it will contain. For example, to declare an immutable integer variable, you can use the following code:

```
let x: i32 = 10;
```

In this case, the variable "x" is a signed 32-bit integer with an initial value of 10. Since this variable has been declared as immutable, its value cannot be changed later in the code.

If you want to declare a mutable variable in Rust, you can use the keyword "mut" before the variable name. For example, to declare a mutable integer variable, you can use the following code:

```
let mut y: i32 = 20;
```

In this case, the variable "y" has been declared as mutable, which means its value can be changed at any point in the subsequent code after its initialization. This flexibility is extremely useful when working with data that needs to be updated or modified during program execution.

A fundamental aspect of variables in Rust is the concept of "ownership," which refers to how Rust manages the memory allocated for variables. In Rust, each variable has an owner, which is responsible for deallocating the memory allocated for the variable when it is no longer in use. This automatic memory management is crucial to ensure the reliability and safety of the system in Rust.

When a variable is assigned to another variable, the ownership of the original variable is transferred to the destination variable. This means that the original variable will no longer be accessible and will be deallocated automatically once the destination variable goes out of the scope in which it was defined. This mechanism of "ownership transfer" is one of the key concepts that make Rust such a safe and robust programming language.

Additionally, Rust also supports the concept of "borrowing," which allows passing a reference to a variable to a function or another part of the code without directly transferring ownership of the variable itself. This mechanism helps avoid issues related to concurrency and memory management, ensuring that variables are used safely and efficiently within the program.

Another important aspect of variables in Rust is error handling, which is crucial to ensure code correctness and system stability. In Rust, errors are handled through the "Result" mechanism, which returns a value of type "Result<T, E>" in case of success or error. This mechanism ensures that any errors are handled elegantly and robustly, ensuring that the program can function reliably even in unexpected situations.

Variables are fundamental elements within a Rust program and play a key role in data management, memory management, and error handling. Through a combination of immutable and mutable variables, ownership and borrowing management, and error handling through the "Result" mechanism, Rust provides developers with a powerful and flexible tool for creating reliable and secure software. Proper understanding and management of variables in Rust are essential to fully leverage the capabilities of this language and write high-quality code that is performant, reliable, and secure.

7.Funzioni e i moduli di Rust

Rust is a powerful systems programming language that focuses on safety, speed, and concurrency. It was created by Mozilla and was first released in 2010. Rust is often praised for its memory safety guarantees, which are enforced at compile time, eliminating the need for a garbage collector. This makes Rust a great choice for developing systems software, embedded applications, and performance-critical software.

One of the key features of Rust is its focus on zero-cost abstractions. This means that high-level abstractions do not come with a performance penalty. In Rust, you can write code that is as high-level and expressive as in other modern programming languages, while still having the performance of low-level languages like C or C++.

In Rust, functions are the building blocks of

the code. Functions in Rust are declared using the `fn` keyword, followed by the function name, parameters, return type, and body of the function. Here is an example of a simple function in Rust:

```
fn greet(name: &str) {
    println!("Hello, {}!", name);
}
```

In this example, the `greet` function takes a string slice `name` as a parameter and prints out a greeting message using the `println!` macro.

Functions in Rust can also return values using the `->` syntax. Here is an example of a function that calculates the square of a number:

```
fn square(num: i32) -> i32 {

    num * num

}
```

You can call the `square` function like this:

```
let result = square(5);

println!("The square of 5 is: {}", result);
```

Rust also supports closures, which are anonymous functions that can capture variables from their enclosing scope. Closures in Rust are defined using the `||` syntax. Here is an example of a closure that adds two numbers:

```
let add = |a, b| a + b;
let result = add(5, 3);
println!("The result of adding 5 and 3 is: {}", result);
```

Modules in Rust allow you to organize your code into separate units of functionality. Modules in Rust are declared using the `mod` keyword, followed by the module name and a block of code containing the module's contents. Here is an example of a module in Rust:

```
mod math {
    pub fn square(num: i32) -> i32 {
```

```
        num * num

    }

}
```

You can use the `math` module like this:

```
let result = math::square(5);

println!("The square of 5 is: {}", result);
```

Modules in Rust can be nested, allowing you to create a hierarchy of modules to organize your code. You can also control the visibility of items within a module using the `pub` keyword. Public items can be accessed from outside the module, while private items are only accessible within the module.

Rust also provides a feature called `use` declarations, which allow you to bring items from a module into scope without having to use the fully qualified name. Here is an example of using a `use` declaration:

```
use math::square;

let result = square(5);

println!("The square of 5 is: {}", result);
```

In addition to functions and modules, Rust also supports traits, which are similar to interfaces in other programming languages. Traits define a set of methods that a type must implement in order to conform to the trait. This allows you to write generic code that can work with different types as long as they implement the required trait.

Here is an example of a trait in Rust:

```
```

trait Area {

    fn area(&self) -> f64;

}

struct Circle {

    radius: f64,

}

impl Area for Circle {

    fn area(&self) -> f64 {

        std::f64::consts::PI * self.radius *
self.radius
```
```

```
    }
}

struct Rectangle {
    width: f64,
    height: f64,
}

impl Area for Rectangle {
    fn area(&self) -> f64 {
        self.width * self.height
    }
}
```

You can use the `Area` trait like this:

```
let circle = Circle { radius: 5.0 };

let rectangle = Rectangle { width: 3.0, height: 4.0 };


println!("The area of the circle is: {}", circle.area());

println!("The area of the rectangle is: {}", rectangle.area());
```

Traits in Rust allow you to write polymorphic code that can work with different types, as long as they implement the required methods. This promotes code reuse and helps write more generic and flexible code.

In conclusion, functions and modules are essential building blocks in Rust that allow you to organize and structure your code. With its focus on safety, speed, and concurrency,

Rust provides a powerful programming language for developing systems software, embedded applications, and performance-critical software. By leveraging functions, modules, and traits, you can write efficient and reliable code in Rust that meets the demands of modern software development.

Modules can also contain variables and classes in addition to functions. For example, a module could include useful constants such as the value of π or the speed of light, which can be imported and used in other programs without having to rewrite them each time. An example of a module that defines a constant for π and a function to calculate the area of a circle would be as follows:

```
```

pi = 3.14159

def area_circle(radius):
```
```

```
    return pi * radius**2
```

```
```

This module could be imported and used in a main program to calculate the area of a circle with a specified radius:

```
```

```
import geometry

radius = 5

area = geometry.area_circle(radius)

print(area)
```

```
```

In this case, the value of π defined in the "geometry" module is used to calculate the area of a circle with a radius of 5.

Modules can also be organized into packages, which are folders containing one or more related modules. A package is a hierarchical structure that allows code to be organized and divided in a more orderly and scalable way, allowing different components of a program to be kept separate.

To create a package, simply create a folder with a special file named "__init__.py", which Python will interpret as a Python package. Within this folder, you can create one or more modules that make up the package, dividing the code into smaller, reusable units.

For example, if we want to create a package called "geometry" containing the modules "circle" and "rectangle" that define functions to calculate the area of their respective geometric shapes, we can organize the package structure as follows:

```
```

```
geometry/

    __init__.py

    circle.py

    rectangle.py
```
```

Inside the "circle.py" and "rectangle.py" files, we can define functions to calculate the area of the circle and rectangle respectively, and then import them into other programs using the syntax "import geometry.circle" and "import geometry.rectangle".

Packages allow code to be organized and structured in related modules, making it easier to manage and maintain complex programs. They can contain any number of modules and packages, allowing for a hierarchical and modular structure to organize and separate code into smaller, reusable units.
```

Functions and modules are two fundamental concepts in programming that allow code to be organized and structured efficiently and reusable. Functions allow a program to be divided into smaller, manageable blocks, making code more readable, maintainable, and reusable. Modules, on the other hand, allow code to be organized and separated into logical and reusable units, allowing complex programs to be divided into more manageable and modular components. By using functions and modules, it is possible to create more organized, scalable programs that are easier to maintain over time.

8.Ownership and borrowing in Rust

Ownership and borrowing are two fundamental concepts in Rust programming language that play a crucial role in managing memory and ensuring memory safety. Understanding these concepts is key to writing efficient and safe Rust code.

Ownership in Rust refers to the rules that govern how memory is managed. In Rust, each value has a variable that owns it. When the owner goes out of scope, the value is dropped and its memory is deallocated. This ensures that there are no memory leaks in Rust programs.

Rust follows the ownership system to determine when memory should be deallocated. When a value is bound to a variable, the variable becomes the owner of that value. Ownership can be transferred from one variable to another using the `move` keyword. This allows Rust to optimize memory usage and improve performance.

One important aspect of ownership in Rust is the concept of borrowing. Borrowing allows a reference to a value to be taken without taking ownership of the value. There are two types of borrowing in Rust: immutable borrowing and mutable borrowing. Immutable borrowing allows multiple references to a value to exist at the same time, but these references cannot be changed. Mutable borrowing allows a single mutable reference to a value, which can be changed.

Borrowing in Rust is enforced by the compiler to prevent data races and ensure memory safety. The Rust compiler performs strict checks at compile time to ensure that borrowing rules are followed. This helps prevent common memory-related bugs such as use-after-free errors, double free errors, and data races.

Ownership and borrowing work together to ensure memory safety and prevent common programming errors. By following Rust's ownership and borrowing rules, developers can write efficient and safe code without worrying about memory management issues.

To better understand ownership and borrowing in Rust, let's look at some examples:

```rust
fn main() {
    let mut s = String::from("Hello, world!");

    // s is the owner of the String value

    // we can pass a reference to s using borrowing

    print_greeting(&s);
```

```rust
    // s is still the owner of the String value

    // we can mutate s by adding more text to it

    s.push_str(", Rust!");


    // s goes out of scope here

    // the String value is dropped and memory
is deallocated
}


fn print_greeting(s: &String) {

    // s is a reference to the String value owned
by s

    println!("{}", s);

}
```

In this example, `s` is the owner of the

`String` value "Hello, world!". We pass a reference to `s` using borrowing in the `print_greeting` function. This allows us to access the `String` value without taking ownership of it. After calling `print_greeting`, we mutate `s` by adding more text to it. Finally, `s` goes out of scope and the `String` value is dropped.

One common pitfall when working with ownership and borrowing in Rust is the issue of dangling references. Dangling references occur when a reference outlives the value it refers to. Rust prevents dangling references by ensuring that references are always valid during their lifetime.

```rust
fn main() {
    let r;

    {
```

```
        let x = 42;

        r = &x; // ERROR: `x` does not live long
enough

    }


    println!("{}", r);

}
```

In this example, `x` is a local variable that goes out of scope at the end of the inner block. The reference `r` outlives `x`, which would result in a dangling reference if allowed. Rust prevents this by giving a compile-time error indicating that `x` does not live long enough.

To overcome the issue of dangling references, Rust introduces the concept of lifetimes. Lifetimes specify the scope in which a reference is valid. By annotating references with lifetimes, developers can ensure that references are always valid and prevent dangling references.

```rust
fn main() {
    let r;

    {
        let x = 42;
        r = &x; // ERROR: `x` does not live long enough
    }

    println!("{}", r);
}
```

By annotating the reference `r` with the

lifetime `'a`, we can specify that the reference is valid for a particular scope. This ensures that the reference does not outlive the value it refers to and prevents dangling references.

Ownership and borrowing in Rust are powerful tools for managing memory and ensuring memory safety. By following Rust's ownership rules and using borrowing correctly, developers can write efficient and safe code without the risk of memory-related bugs. Understanding these concepts is essential for mastering Rust programming and building robust applications.

9. Error handling in Rust

How Rust handles errors and the various techniques and tools available to handle them effectively.

Before delving into how Rust handles errors, it is important to understand what is meant by an error in a program. An error can be caused by various factors, such as invalid input, a system call failure, memory errors, or programming errors. Handling errors effectively is crucial to ensuring the stability and security of our software.

In Rust, errors can be managed using two main mechanisms: results and panics. Results are a data type that represents the result of an operation that can fail. A result can be of two types: Ok, which represents a valid result, and Err, which represents an error. When a function returns a result of type Result, the caller can check whether the operation was successful or if an error occurred.

For example, consider the following function that divides two numbers and returns a result of type Result:

```rust
fn divide(a: i32, b: i32) -> Result<i32, String> {
    if b == 0 {
        Err("Cannot divide by zero".to_string())
    } else {
        Ok(a / b)
    }
}
```

In the above code, the divide function returns a Result<i32, String>, where the Ok type represents the division result and the Err type represents an error message in case the divisor is zero. The caller can handle the error returned by the divide function and act accordingly.

A panic, on the other hand, represents an unrecoverable error that immediately halts program execution. Panics are automatically raised when a critically unhandleable error occurs, such as an out-of-bounds access or an arithmetic overflow. Panics are very rare in Rust and are only used for severe errors that cannot be safely handled.

In addition to results and panics, Rust also offers the Option data type, which represents an optional value. An Option value can be Some, representing a valid value, or None, representing the absence of a value. Optionals are particularly useful when representing a result that may or may not be present.

```rust
fn divide(a: i32, b: i32) -> Option<i32> {
    if b == 0 {
        None
    } else {
        Some(a / b)
    }
}
```

In the code above, the divide function returns a value of type Option<i32> that represents the division result if the divisor is not zero, otherwise it returns None.

Apart from the data types available in Rust for error handling, Rust also provides a wide range of features to handle errors safely and efficiently. One of the most important features of Rust is pattern matching, which allows for elegant handling of results and panics.

Pattern matching enables writing clearer and more concise code to handle errors effectively. For example, consider the following example of using pattern matching to handle a Result type:

```rust
fn divide(a: i32, b: i32) -> Result<i32, String> {
    if b == 0 {
        Err("Cannot divide by zero".to_string())
    } else {
        Ok(a / b)
    }
}

fn main() {
```

```rust
    let result = divide(10, 5);


    match result {

        Ok(value) => println!("The result is {}",
value),

        Err(error) => println!("An error occurred:
{}", error),

    }

}

```

In the previous code, the division function
returns a Result<i32, String> type result that
is handled through pattern matching in the
main function. If the division operation is
successful, the result is printed to the screen,
otherwise an error message is printed.

In addition to pattern matching, Rust also
offers the concept of error handlers which
allow centralized and uniform error handling
throughout the code. Error handlers allow for

custom error handling and provide detailed information about the causes of errors.

To create a custom error handler in Rust, the std::error::Error trait can be used to define a data type representing a custom error. For example, consider the following example of creating a custom error handler in Rust:

```rust
use std::error::Error;

use std::fmt;


#[derive(Debug)]

struct DivisionByZero;


impl fmt::Display for DivisionByZero {

    fn fmt(&self, f: &mut fmt::Formatter) -> fmt::Result {
```

```rust
        write!(f, "Cannot divide by zero")
    }
}


impl Error for DivisionByZero {}


fn division(a: i32, b: i32) -> Result<i32,
DivisionByZero> {
    if b == 0 {
        Err(DivisionByZero)
    } else {
        Ok(a / b)
    }
}


fn main() {
    let result = division(10, 0);
```

```
    match result {

        Ok(value) => println!("The result is {}",
value),

        Err(error) => println!("An error occurred:
{}", error),

    }

}
```

In the example above, we defined a custom error handler called DivisionByZero which represents the case where division by zero is attempted. The error handler implements the std::error::Error trait to provide detailed error information and is used in the division function to handle the case where the divisor is zero.

In addition to error handling using results, panics, pattern matching, and error handlers,

Rust also offers the ability to handle errors asynchronously using the async/await system. Async/await is a feature of Rust that allows for writing asynchronous code in a concise and readable manner.

To handle errors asynchronously in Rust, the std::future::Future trait can be used to represent an asynchronous operation that may fail. A Future returns a result of type Result<Option<T>, E> where T is the type of the returned value and E is the type of the error. By using async/await, asynchronous code can be written without having to manually manage threads and callbacks.

```rust
use std::future::Future;


async fn division(a: i32, b: i32) -> Result<i32, &'static str> {

    if b == 0 {
```

```rust
        Err("Cannot divide by zero")
    } else {
        Ok(a / b)
    }
}


#[tokio::main]
async fn main() {
    let result = division(10, 0).await;

    match result {
        Ok(value) => println!("The result is {}", value),

        Err(error) => println!("An error occurred: {}", error),
    }
}
```

In the above example, we defined an asynchronous division function that returns a Result<i32, &'static str> type result and use async/await to handle the function asynchronously. By utilizing the std::future::Future trait and async/await, errors in asynchronous code can be effectively managed in Rust.

Lastly, another important tool for error handling in Rust is the ownership management mechanism which allows for safe and efficient memory management. Thanks to the ownership management mechanism, Rust ensures that each value has a single owner and that memory is deallocated correctly once the value is no longer in use.

The ownership management mechanism helps to avoid common errors such as double memory deallocation or using memory after deallocation. Through this mechanism, Rust offers excellent memory management safety and reduces the risk of memory-related programming errors.

Rust provides a wide range of tools and techniques for handling errors safely and efficiently. By using results, panics, pattern matching, error handlers, async/await, and the ownership management mechanism, errors can be handled elegantly, reducing the risk of programming errors in our software. Error handling in Rust is one of the strengths of this language, contributing to the safety and stability of software developed with Rust.

10.Traits and Generics in Rust

Rust is a powerful and modern programming language that emphasizes safety, performance, and concurrency. One of the key features of Rust is its strong type system, which allows developers to write robust and efficient code. In this article, we will explore two important concepts in Rust: Traits and Generics.

Traits in Rust are similar to interfaces in other programming languages, such as Java or C#. They define a set of methods that a type must implement in order to satisfy the trait. Traits allow developers to write generic code that can work with multiple types, as long as those types implement the required methods.

Generics, on the other hand, allow developers to write code that can work with different types without sacrificing type safety. With generics, developers can create reusable functions and data structures that can be used with any type that meets the constraints defined by the generic type parameters.

Now, let's delve deeper into Traits and Generics in Rust and see how they can be used to write elegant and efficient code.

1. Traits:

Traits in Rust are similar to interfaces in other programming languages, but with some key differences. In Rust, traits are used to define a set of methods that a type must implement in order to satisfy the trait. Traits are declared using the `trait` keyword, followed by the trait name and a set of method signatures.

For example, let's define a trait named `Printable` that requires a type to implement a `print` method:

```
trait Printable {

    fn print(&self);

}
```

To implement a trait for a specific type, we use the `impl` keyword followed by the trait name:

```
struct Person {

    name: String,

    age: u32,

}

impl Printable for Person {

    fn print(&self) {
```

```
    println!("Name: {}, Age: {}", self.name,
self.age);

  }

}
```
```

Now, any type that implements the `Printable` trait can be used with functions that expect a `Printable` type. This allows developers to write generic code that can work with multiple types, as long as those types implement the required methods.

2. Generics:

Generics in Rust allow developers to write code that can work with different types without sacrificing type safety. Generics are declared using angle brackets (`<>`) followed by one or more type parameters.
```

For example, let's create a generic function named `max` that finds the maximum value in a list of values:

```
```

fn max<T: PartialOrd>(list: &[T]) ->
Option<&T> {

    if list.is_empty() {

        return None;

    }

    let mut max_value = &list[0];

    for value in list {

        if value > max_value {

            max_value = value;

        }

    }
```
```

```
    Some(max_value)

}
```

In this example, the `max` function takes a slice of values of any type that implements the `PartialOrd` trait, which defines the `>` operator for comparison. The function returns an `Option` containing a reference to the maximum value in the list.

Generics allow developers to create reusable functions and data structures that can work with any type that meets the constraints defined by the generic type parameters. This promotes code reuse and reduces code duplication, leading to more maintainable and scalable codebases.

3. Benefits of Traits and Generics:

Traits and generics are powerful features in Rust that offer several benefits to developers:

- Type Safety: Traits and generics in Rust ensure type safety by enforcing compile-time checks on the types used in generic code. This helps prevent runtime errors caused by type mismatches or invalid operations.

- Code Reusability: Traits and generics allow developers to write generic code that can work with multiple types, reducing code duplication and promoting code reuse. This leads to more maintainable and scalable codebases.

- Polymorphism: Traits in Rust enable polymorphism by allowing different types to implement the same set of methods. This promotes code flexibility and extensibility, as new types can be added without modifying existing code.

- Performance: Generics in Rust are monomorphized, meaning that generic functions and data structures are specialized at compile time for each concrete type used. This eliminates the runtime overhead associated with generic code in other programming languages.

- Expressiveness: Traits and generics in Rust enable developers to write expressive and concise code that captures the essence of the problem domain. This leads to code that is easier to understand, debug, and maintain.

4. Examples of Traits and Generics in Rust:

Let's explore some examples of how Traits and Generics can be used in Rust to write elegant and efficient code:

Traits and generics are powerful features in Rust that offer several benefits to developers:

- Type Safety: Traits and generics in Rust ensure type safety by enforcing compile-time checks on the types used in generic code. This helps prevent runtime errors caused by type mismatches or invalid operations.

- Code Reusability: Traits and generics allow developers to write generic code that can work with multiple types, reducing code duplication and promoting code reuse. This leads to more maintainable and scalable codebases.

- Polymorphism: Traits in Rust enable polymorphism by allowing different types to implement the same set of methods. This promotes code flexibility and extensibility, as new types can be added without modifying existing code.

- Performance: Generics in Rust are monomorphized, meaning that generic functions and data structures are specialized at compile time for each concrete type used. This eliminates the runtime overhead associated with generic code in other programming languages.

- Expressiveness: Traits and generics in Rust enable developers to write expressive and concise code that captures the essence of the problem domain. This leads to code that is easier to understand, debug, and maintain.

4. Examples of Traits and Generics in Rust:

Let's explore some examples of how Traits and Generics can be used in Rust to write elegant and efficient code:

- Trait Example:

```
```

trait Animal {
    fn speak(&self);
}

struct Dog {
    name: String,
}

impl Animal for Dog {
    fn speak(&self) {
        println!("{} says woof!", self.name);
    }
}
```
```

```
fn main() {

    let dog = Dog { name:
String::from("Rover") };

    dog.speak();

}
```
```

In this example, we define an `Animal` trait
with a `speak` method that must be
implemented by types that satisfy the trait. We
then implement the `Animal` trait for a `Dog`
type and define how a `Dog` should speak.


- Generics Example:


```

fn print_values<T: std::fmt::Debug>(value1:
T, value2: T) {

    println!("Value 1: {:?}, Value 2: {:?}",
value1, value2);
```
```

```
}

fn main() {

    print_values(42, 3.14);

    print_values("hello", "world");

}
```
```

In this example, we define a generic function named `print_values` that takes two values of the same type and prints them using the `Debug` trait for pretty printing. We then call the function with integer and float values, as well as string values, demonstrating the flexibility and reuse of generic code.


5. Conclusion:


Traits and Generics are powerful features in Rust that enable developers to write elegant,
```

efficient, and type-safe code. Traits allow developers to define a set of methods that types must implement, promoting code reuse and polymorphism. Generics allow developers to write reusable functions and data structures that can work with different types, without sacrificing type safety or performance.

By mastering Traits and Generics in Rust, developers can write expressive and concise code that is easy to understand, debug, and maintain. These features are essential tools in the Rust developer's toolbox and are key to harnessing the full potential of the language. Start exploring Traits and Generics in Rust to write robust and efficient code for your next project. Happy coding!

11.Concurrency and parallelism in Rust

Concurrency and parallelism in Rust

Concurrency and parallelism are two crucial concepts in modern programming, especially when it comes to building high-performance applications. Rust, a systems programming language known for its safety and speed, provides powerful tools and features for handling concurrency and parallelism efficiently.

Concurrency refers to the ability of a system to run multiple tasks at the same time. This allows programs to perform multiple operations simultaneously, improving efficiency and responsiveness. On the other hand, parallelism involves executing multiple tasks simultaneously using multiple CPUs or processor cores, which can significantly increase performance.

In Rust, concurrency and parallelism are achieved through two main constructs: threads and async/await. Let's dive deeper into how these features work and how they can be effectively used in Rust programming.

Threads in Rust

Threads are lightweight units of execution that allow a program to run multiple tasks concurrently. Rust provides a powerful threading model based on the `std::thread` module, which allows developers to create and manage threads easily.

To create a new thread in Rust, you can use the `std::thread::spawn` function, which takes a closure representing the code to be executed in the new thread. Here's an example demonstrating how to spawn a new thread in Rust:

```rust
```

```rust
use std::thread;

fn main() {
    let handle = thread::spawn(|| {
        println!("Hello from a thread!");
    });

    handle.join().unwrap();
}
```

In this example, a new thread is spawned to print a message, "Hello from a thread!". The `join()` method is called on the thread handle to wait for the thread to finish executing before proceeding further.

Rust's type system ensures that data shared between threads is safe and free from data races. You can use synchronization primitives like mutexes, channels, and atomic types to coordinate access to shared data between threads.

Async/await in Rust

Async/await is a powerful feature introduced in Rust that allows developers to write asynchronous code in a synchronous style. It simplifies the complexity of dealing with callbacks and event loops when working with asynchronous operations.

To use async/await in Rust, you need to mark functions and blocks of code as asynchronous using the `async` keyword. By using the `await` keyword inside async functions, you can pause the execution of asynchronous tasks until the awaited operation is complete.

Here's an example demonstrating how async/await can be used in Rust:

```rust
use tokio::time::sleep;
use std::time::Duration;

async fn async_function() {
    println!("Before sleep");
    sleep(Duration::from_secs(2)).await;
    println!("After sleep");
}

#[tokio::main]
async fn main() {
    async_function().await;
}
```

In this example, the `async_function` sleeps for 2 seconds using `tokio`'s async runtime. The `main` function marks the entry point as asynchronous and awaits the result of `async_function` before terminating.

Concurrency and parallelism in Rust

Combining threads and async/await, Rust provides a powerful concurrency and parallelism model that allows developers to build efficient and scalable applications. By leveraging these features, you can write performant code that takes advantage of multi-core processors and high levels of concurrency.

Rust's `tokio` and `async-std` libraries are popular choices for building asynchronous applications, providing tools for handling complex asynchronous tasks, networking, and I/O operations.

Additionally, Rust's type system and ownership model ensure that code is safe and free from common concurrency issues like data races and deadlocks. The `Send` and `Sync` traits enable data to be safely shared between threads and tasks.

When designing concurrent and parallel systems in Rust, it's essential to consider factors like task scheduling, synchronization, and resource management. Using tools like `crossbeam`, `rayon`, and `futures` can help simplify the development of concurrent applications in Rust.

Conclusion

Rust provides a robust set of features and tools for handling concurrency and parallelism effectively. By leveraging threads, async/await, and asynchronous libraries like `tokio` and `async-std`, developers can write high-performance, scalable applications in Rust.

Concurrency and parallelism are essential concepts to master when building modern software systems, and Rust's safety guarantees and performance optimizations make it an ideal choice for developing concurrent and parallel applications.

By understanding how to use threads, async/await, and synchronization primitives in Rust, developers can unlock the full potential of multi-core processors and build efficient, responsive applications. Whether you're building a web server, a distributed system, or a data processing pipeline, Rust's concurrency and parallelism features are sure to help you achieve your performance goals.

12. Rust and conditional constructs

One of the key features of Rust is its rich set of control flow constructs, including conditional statements such as if, else if, and match. In this article, we will explore the use of conditional constructs in Rust and how they can be leveraged to write more efficient and robust code.

The if statement is one of the most basic control flow constructs in Rust. It takes a boolean expression and executes a block of code if the expression evaluates to true. Here is a simple example of an if statement in Rust:

```rust
fn main() {
    let x = 5;

    if x < 10 {
```

```
        println!("x is less than 10");

    }

}
```

In this example, we declare a variable x with a value of 5 and use an if statement to check if x is less than 10. If the condition is true, the message "x is less than 10" is printed to the console.

Rust also supports the else if construct, which allows for multiple conditional branches to be evaluated. Here is an example that demonstrates the use of else if in Rust:

```rust
fn main() {
    let x = 15;
```

```
    if x < 10 {

        println!("x is less than 10");

    } else if x < 20 {

        println!("x is between 10 and 20");

    } else {

        println!("x is greater than or equal to
20");

    }

}
```

In this example, we check if x is less than 10, between 10 and 20, or greater than or equal to 20, and print the corresponding message based on the condition.

Another powerful conditional construct in Rust is match, which allows for exhaustive pattern matching. It can be used to match against multiple patterns and execute different code based on the matched pattern. Here is an example of match in Rust:

```rust
fn main() {
    let x = 5;

    match x {
        1 => println!("x is one"),
        2 => println!("x is two"),
        3 | 4 | 5 => println!("x is three, four, or five"),
        _ => println!("x is something else"),
    }
}
```

In this example, we match against the value of

x and print a different message based on the matched pattern. The underscore (_) is a wildcard pattern that matches any value not covered by the previous patterns.

One of the benefits of using match in Rust is that it enforces exhaustiveness checking, which means that the compiler will ensure that all possible cases are handled. This can help prevent bugs related to missing or incorrect handling of certain cases.

In addition to if, else if, and match, Rust also provides a few other conditional constructs such as while loops, for loops, and the loop statement. While loops iterate as long as a condition is true, for loops iterate over a range or an iterator, and the loop statement creates an infinite loop until a break statement is encountered.

Overall, Rust's rich set of conditional constructs make it a powerful language for writing safe and efficient code. By leveraging these constructs effectively, developers can ensure that their code is robust and handles all possible scenarios. Whether you are writing a small script or a complex application, Rust's control flow constructs provide the tools needed to build reliable software.

Index

www.ingramcontent.com/pod-product-compliance
Lightning Source LLC
LaVergne TN
LVHW051702050326
832903LV00032B/3950